GLOBAL EFFECTS

THE IMPACT OF SCIENCE, TECHNOLOGY, AND ECONOMICS
IN SOUTH ASIA

PETER KOGLER

PowerKiDS
press

Published in 2021 by The Rosen Publishing Group, Inc.
29 East 21st Street, New York, NY 10010

First Edition

Editor: Siyavush Saidian
Book Design: Tanya Dellaccio

Photo Credits: Cover, pp. 17, 21 (both) NurPhoto/Getty Images; p. 5 PSboom/Shutterstock.com; p. 7 Bloomberg/Getty Images; p. 9 (both) SNEHIT PHOTO/Shutterstock.com; p. 10 klempa/Shutterstock.com; p. 13 Travel Stock/Shutterstock.com; p. 14 The India Today Group/Getty Images; p. 15 Gerhard Joren/ LightRocket/Getty Images; p 19 Jeff Greenberg/Universal Images Group/Getty Images; p. 23 Sharad Raval/Shutterstock.com; p. 25 (both) STRDEL/AFP/Getty Images; p. 28 Dmitry Chulov/Shutterstock.com; p. 29 jannoon028/Shutterstock.com.

Cataloging-in-Publication Data
Names: Kogler, Peter.
Title: The impact of science, technology, and economics in South Asia / Peter Kogler.
Description: New York : PowerKids Press, 2021. | Series: Global effects | Includes glossary and index.
Identifiers: ISBN 9781725322486 (pbk.) | ISBN 9781725322509 (library bound) | ISBN 9781725322493 (6 pack) | ISBN 9781725322516 (ebook)
Subjects: LCSH: South Asia–Juvenile literature. | Technology–South Asia. | Science–South Asia.
Classification: LCC DS335.K64 2021 | DDC 954–dc23

Manufactured in the United States of America

CPSIA Compliance Information: Batch #CSPK20: For Further Information contact Rosen Publishing, New York, New York at 1-800-237-9932

Find us on

CONTENTS

WELCOME TO SOUTH ASIA

The region of South Asia is made up of eight nations, each with a unique history and culture. These nations are Pakistan, Afghanistan, Bangladesh, Sri Lanka, Bhutan, Maldives, Nepal, and India. With a population of nearly 2 billion people, this region is home to a wide variety of cultures, governments, and industries. It is also happens to be one of the world's fastest-growing regions. While South Asia's overall **infrastructure** is considered somewhat weak, its health and education industries are improving.

The area's economy is largely dependent on the use of natural resources—but this could spell trouble in the future. Non-renewable resources are trending downward as the world shifts to cleaner energy. However, if improvements can be made in South Asia's technology and infrastructure, its countries could create new industries that don't rely on natural resources. New industries will strengthen the economy.

FAST FACT

AS CITIES GROW LARGER AND TALLER ACROSS SOUTH ASIA, NATURAL DISASTERS BECOME MORE DEADLY. THE REGION'S FREQUENT EARTHQUAKES ARE ESPECIALLY DANGEROUS, AS THEY CAN CAUSE BUILDINGS TO COLLAPSE.

NATURAL DISASTERS

South Asia often finds itself the victim of a variety of natural disasters. These disasters include **monsoons**, **tsunamis**, **typhoons**, and earthquakes. Due to the high poverty rates among the region's 1.8 billion people, many do not have the resources to stay protected during a disaster. Climate change is believed to be a big factor in the rise of natural disasters. This is largely due to a rising sea level, which increases the risk of floods.

THE POPULATION IN SOUTH ASIA HAS SEEN A STEADY INCREASE OVER THE YEARS. THIS IS DUE TO IMPROVING EDUCATION, STRONGER INDUSTRIES, BETTER HEALTH CARE, AND A GROWING ECONOMY.

TYPHOON: A SEVERE TROPICAL STORM CHARACTERIZED BY HIGH WINDS THAT ORIGINATES IN THE INDIAN OCEAN OR WESTERN PACIFIC OCEAN.

TSUNAMI: A LARGE OCEAN WAVE THAT IS CAUSED BY AN EARTHQUAKE ALONG THE FLOOR OF THE OCEAN.

MONSOON: SEASONAL WINDS THAT AFFECT CLIMATE IN THE SOUTHERN AREAS OF ASIA, RESULTING IN WET SPRING AND SUMMER MONTHS AND DRY WINTER MONTHS.

INTERNATIONAL TRADE

South Asia's countries **export** and trade their goods and products across the entire world. In 2017, the region's total exports were valued at nearly $329 billion. The United States, the United Arab Emirates, and China are some of the region's biggest partners in trade.

Clothing and **textiles** are among the region's largest exports. These are products like linen sheets, sweaters, and suits that are produced in Bangladesh and Pakistan. In India, the largest export is **refined** petroleum, or fuel. These products can be created thanks to the **import** of **raw materials** from other countries. Raw cotton, raw metals, and raw fuel are turned into new, usable products in South Asia.

Trade creates an important cycle that helps build the economies of all countries involved. Without raw materials, new products cannot be manufactured, traded, or sold.

RAW MATERIAL: A BASIC THING USED TO BUILD OR CREATE SOMETHING.

FAST FACT

INDIA IS ALSO WELL KNOWN FOR ITS JEWELRY TRADE, WHICH INCLUDES DIAMONDS AND GOLD. IMPORTED DIAMONDS AND GOLD ARE TURNED INTO JEWELRY TO EXPORT AROUND THE WORLD.

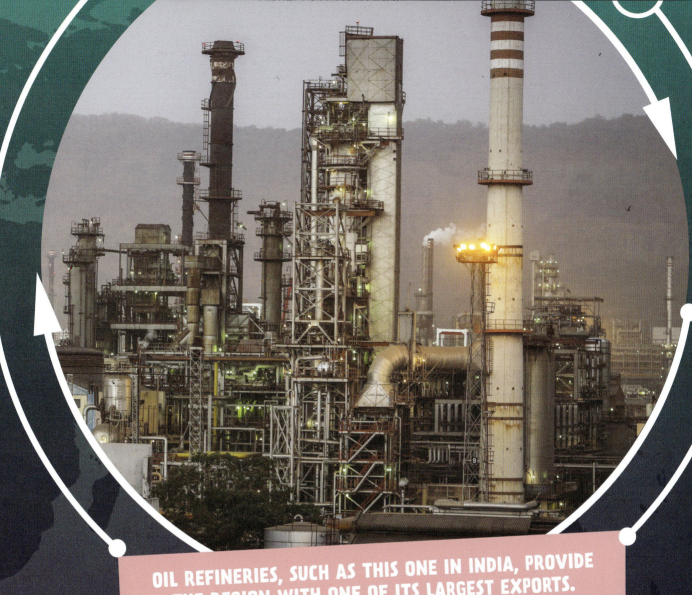

OIL REFINERIES, SUCH AS THIS ONE IN INDIA, PROVIDE THE REGION WITH ONE OF ITS LARGEST EXPORTS.

WAR AND TRADE

In addition to international trade, business also occurs between nations within South Asia, such as Pakistan and Afghanistan. These nations, however, aren't always friendly with each other. This is a result of politics and war that have affected some countries for years. In 2017, trade between Pakistan and Afghanistan declined by more than 25 percent. In July 2019, both nations agreed to work on an existing trade agreement called the Afghanistan-Pakistan Transit Trade Agreement (APTTA). This is expected to increase **commerce** between the two countries.

WHO MAKES UP SOUTH ASIA?

Nearly 2 billion people call South Asia home—and about 25 percent of the world's population lives there. India, Pakistan, and Bangladesh are South Asia's most highly populated regions.

Life expectancy, or how long the average person in an area lives, can be used to measure a region's social, economic, and technological health. In South Asia, men live to about 68 years old, and women live to about 71 years old. Compared to other regions in Asia, South Asia has the lowest life expectancy. However, some countries, including Sri Lanka and Maldives, are becoming more developed.

As the region's development increases, so do infrastructure, health care, and education. This leads to longer life spans, higher birth rates, and a stronger economy. All are expected to increase, along with the South Asian population, over the coming decades.

FAST FACT

CLIMATE CHANGE IS HARMING MANY SOUTH ASIAN COUNTRIES, CAUSING MILLIONS OF PEOPLE TO LEAVE. MANY ARE MOVING WITHIN THE REGION—ESPECIALLY TO INDIA. THESE **MIGRATION** PATTERNS WILL AFFECT THE AREA'S ECONOMIES FOR DECADES TO COME.

MIGRATION: THE MOVEMENT OF GROUPS OF PEOPLE FROM ONE PLACE TO ANOTHER.

THE YOUNGEST NATION IN THE WORLD

By the year 2030, it's possible that India could be the "youngest" nation in the world. Nearly 70 percent of the population there will be of working age (between 15 and 64). This could be good news for India—as long as the government plans for it. As the population gets younger, there must be more jobs available to keep people employed. Modern businesses also require highly skilled workers, which—in India—have historically been male. However, the 2010s saw improvement in many areas of women's rights, which has the opportunity to strengthen the country's economy.

HYDERABAD, INDIA, IS THE NATION'S FOURTH-MOST POPULATED CITY. AS SOUTH ASIA'S POPULATION RISES, CITIES, ECONOMIES, AND TECHNOLOGY MUST ALSO GROW.

BUILDING UP THE ECONOMY

Since the 2000's, South Asia's **gross domestic product (GDP)** has grown increasingly fast. In 2018, the region's overall GDP was nearly $3.5 trillion. Every nation grows its economy differently.

Afghanistan has made improvements within its farming industry, which increases production. Bhutan has done the same with its **hydropower** and **tourism** industries. Increased construction and tourism in Nepal will also grow its overall GDP. The government of Maldives has invested in its tourism industry, supporting construction and transportation projects. These are expected to provide a boost to both tourism and the overall economy.

Elsewhere in South Asia, Sri Lanka and Afghanistan are working together to overcome the economic setbacks that have affected the region. The first meeting of the Sri Lanka-Afghanistan Parliamentary Friendship Association—an alliance between both governments—was held in 2019.

FAST FACT

MALDIVES IS THE RICHEST REGION IN SOUTH ASIA, THANKS TO ITS BEACHES AND A TOURISM INDUSTRY THAT PULLS IN $325 MILLION EVERY YEAR.

GROWING PAINS

South Asia's population, school enrollment, and life expectancy have all grown alongside the region's economy. These are signs that the region is developing at a steady pace. However, there is another factor in South Asia increasing with the rest: pollution. Increased **emissions** are another sign of development, but it's not exactly a good one. More industries and more vehicles on the road lead to more pollution, which is often less regulated in developing countries.

EMISSION: POLLUTION RELEASED INTO THE AIR, ESPECIALLY FROM FACTORIES AND VEHICLES.

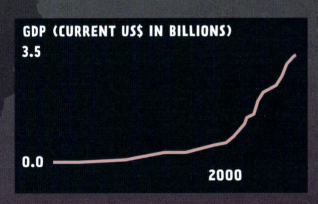

GDP (CURRENT US$ IN BILLIONS)
3.5
0.0
2000

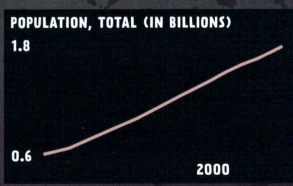

POPULATION, TOTAL (IN BILLIONS)
1.8
0.6
2000

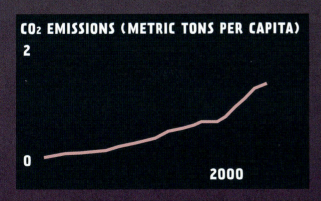

CO_2 EMISSIONS (METRIC TONS PER CAPITA)
2
0
2000

A GROWING GDP MEANS MORE JOBS, MORE WORKERS, AND LONGER LIFE SPANS AS HEALTH CARE AND EDUCATION INCREASE. HOWEVER, POLLUTION ALSO RISES IN A GROWING ECONOMY.

SERVICE INDUSTRIES IN SOUTH ASIA

South Asian industry doesn't only focus on **manufacturing** and exporting. India, for example, is a more service-based economy. In other words, many Indian workers perform services such as **information technology (IT)**, hospital jobs, and even jobs in tourism. Similarly strong service industries can be found in Pakistan, Sri Lanka, and Maldives.

Compared to highly developed countries like the United States, South Asia still has room to improve. Its service industries are a strong start, and skilled workers fill the workforce. These industries help the economy grow. However, India is the only nation in the area with technology and development similar to other major nations. As the global economy continues to favor technology and new industries, South Asian countries will have to adapt to keep up.

INFORMATION TECHNOLOGY (IT): THE STUDY AND USE OF COMPUTERS AND COMPUTER DATA.

MANUFACTURING: BUSINESSES THAT PRODUCE CONSUMER PRODUCTS.

FAST FACT

THE INDIAN GOVERNMENT HAS RECOGNIZED HOW IMPORTANT ITS SERVICE INDUSTRIES ARE—AND HOW IMPORTANT IT WILL BE TO EXPAND THE ECONOMY IN OTHER AREAS. IT IS LOOKING TO INCREASE MANUFACTURING AND HIGH-LEVEL IT JOBS IN THE FUTURE.

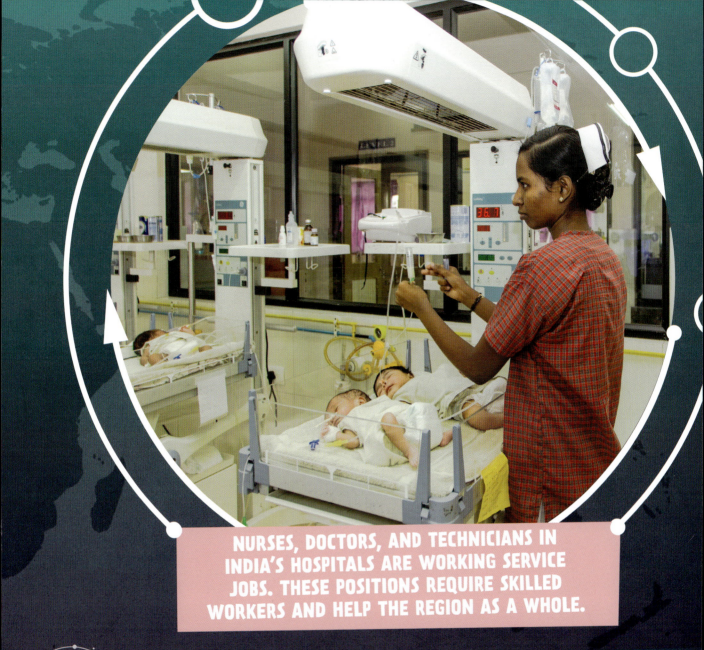

NURSES, DOCTORS, AND TECHNICIANS IN INDIA'S HOSPITALS ARE WORKING SERVICE JOBS. THESE POSITIONS REQUIRE SKILLED WORKERS AND HELP THE REGION AS A WHOLE.

GLOBAL COOPERATION

International trade is an important part of building a global economy. By importing raw materials and exporting finished products, South Asia is a major contributor to worldwide growth. Some South Asian countries, including Afghanistan, have faced economic trouble over the past decades. However, the region is growing more stable every year. As economies grow, other countries and businesses invest money into South Asian industries. This creates even more growth and continues the cycle of economic partnership.

WHAT THE LAND PROVIDES

Natural resources available in South Asia include minerals, forests, and food. Wood and bamboo from South Asian forests are used in products around the world. Precious stones, including diamonds and sapphires, come from India and Sri Lanka, respectively, though India's gemstone production has slowed down in recent decades. South Asia's natural resources aren't just used for trade. They're also used to support its growing cities and expanding populations. India, which produced $1.2 billion worth of iron ore in 2018, used the resource in its own steel industry. Indians also mine coal and petroleum, which powers the region.

Fishing is also a major South Asian industry, and many people rely on fish for food. The entire region, however, is growing. This means demand for both energy and food will continue to increase.

FAST FACT

INDIA PRODUCES ABOUT 40 PERCENT OF THE WORLD'S MANGOES, MAKING IT THE WORLD'S BIGGEST EXPORTER OF THE FRUIT.

A GROWING PROBLEM

Deforestation is threatening one of South Asia's most valuable resources. Deforestation occurs when humans clear out forests. This is done to make room for the cities and farms needed to support the region's growing population. Forests are also cleared so businesses can produce more coal, oil, and gemstones—all of which are important to the overall economy. However, deforestation contributes to global warming and harms natural habitats.

FISH, WHICH ARE AN IMPORTANT NATURAL RESOURCE IN MALDIVES, ARE CONSIDERED RENEWABLE. HOWEVER, OVERFISHING—CATCHING TOO MANY FISH BEFORE THE POPULATION RENEWS—IS A THREAT TO THE INDUSTRY.

THE SOUTH ASIAN WORKFORCE

More men than women are members of the South Asian workforce. In fact, female employment rates in India, Bhutan, and Sri Lanka declined each year between 2005 and 2015, even as these economies grew. This is partially because men in poorer families benefited from economic growth and received higher pay, meaning their wives no longer had to work.

Businesses from other countries continue to add jobs to the South Asian economy through **outsourcing**. This practice is popular because companies can pay workers in this region less than they'd have to pay workers from their home countries.

Child workers are an important part of many South Asian economies. Across the region there are nearly 30 million children in employment. This includes children who work in family labor, such as farming, to provide food.

OUTSOURCING: MOVING JOBS FROM ONE COUNTRY TO ANOTHER.

FAST FACT

THERE ARE TENS OF MILLIONS OF OUT-OF-SCHOOL CHILDREN IN SOUTH ASIA. AS COUNTRIES IN THE REGION DEVELOP, INTERNATIONAL ORGANIZATIONS ENCOURAGE GOVERNMENTS TO INVEST IN EDUCATION FOR CHILDREN.

IMPROVING SAFETY IN INDIA

Factories and other industrial workplaces in India can be dangerous places. In 2016, 13 Indian garment workers died when their factory caught fire. Unlike in highly developed nations, India does not have many national laws that address dangerous workplaces. Organizations, such as the International Labor Organization (ILO), are trying to improve **occupational** safety in the country. The ILO works alongside the government to develop stronger regulations and make sure the rules are being followed.

IT IS NOT UNUSUAL TO SEE CHILD LABORERS IN SOUTH ASIA. MANY HAVE TO WORK TO SUPPORT THEIR FAMILIES AND THEMSELVES.

CAPITAL OF THE REGION

In 2017, the South Asian economy grew by 7 percent. Compared to already-developed nations—which grow from 1 to 2 percent each year—this region is changing quickly. The growing economy has been the result of lots of investment. **Capital** has been put toward better schools, improved health care, and advanced technology. Infrastructure, such as electricity, factories, and roads, has also been improved.

Sources of capital in South Asia are mixed. Maldives, for instance, has strong tourism, trade, and fishing markets. These markets have helped the small island nation become the richest in South Asia. Bhutan depends on its forestry and farming industries for capital. Bhutan, though, has less-developed infrastructure. The lack of a strong infrastructure puts stress on its industries and capital.

CAPITAL: THE INCOME THAT A REGION PRODUCES AND USES FOR ITS GROWTH AND DEVELOPMENT.

FAST FACT

BY 2030, IT'S POSSIBLE INDIA WILL BE THE THIRD-LARGEST ECONOMY IN THE WORLD. CAPITAL INVESTMENT HAS ALREADY BOOSTED ITS GDP, WHICH IS EXPECTED TO CONTINUE GROWING.

INTERNATIONAL CORPORATIONS LIKE MCDONALD'S PROVIDE JOBS FOR SOUTH ASIANS. IF THESE BUSINESSES SUCCEED, MORE MONEY IS INVESTED IN THE REGION, WHICH CREATES EVEN MORE JOBS.

GROWING THE GLOBAL ECONOMY

A growing number of international companies are investing their money in South Asia. These investments are an important source of capital in the region. Created in 2014, the Make in India program encourages foreign corporations to open factories and businesses in the country. These companies provide manufacturing jobs and help the economy thrive. Make in India has been successful in its early years, convincing corporations like Foxconn ($5 billion) and Kia Motors ($1 billion) to invest capital in the country's manufacturing future.

SOUTH ASIAN ENTREPRENEURS

The culture in some South Asian nations makes it hard to become an **entrepreneur**. Starting a business is very risky, and parents prefer their children work traditional jobs. However, many young people are influenced by successful businesses in the United States—especially in the technology industry. IT is already a popular field in the region, and there are countless start-ups (or new businesses), each trying to come up with the next big idea like Facebook or Instagram.

Despite its popularity, however, not all entrepreneurs work in the tech industry. Shamama Arbab runs her own company—Euro Industries—in Pakistan's food industry. South Asia has historically not produced many female entrepreneurs, though organizations like South Asia Women's Entrepreneurship Symposium are connecting businesswomen with resources to succeed.

ENTREPRENEUR: A PERSON WHO STARTS THEIR OWN BUSINESS.

FAST FACT

ONLINE SHOPPING IN INDIA IS MOSTLY DONE THROUGH FLIPKART, A COMPANY FOUNDED IN 2007 BY TWO INDIAN ENTREPRENEURS.

INDIA'S FILM INDUSTRY ATTRACTS ENTREPRENEURS, CREATES JOBS, AND PROVIDES CAPITAL WHEN MOVIES ARE CREATED AND RELEASED.

MOVE OVER, HOLLYWOOD

Bollywood—India's huge film industry—is an important piece of the nation's economy. In 2016, it added more than $4 billion to the nation's GDP. It's also attracted many entrepreneurs to the business of filmmaking. For example, someone skilled in video editing or script writing can help a studio improve its on-screen products. For the industry to grow, people need to know about its movies. From website design to advertising, Bollywood has become a top destination for India's talented youth. These entrepreneurs work together to get Bollywood's films out into the world.

TECHNOLOGICAL INNOVATIONS

As the South Asian economy and region grows, its technology must also improve. Some nations in the region, such as Pakistan, need help to catch up. China has invested billions of dollars as part of the China-Pakistan Economic Corridor project, which aims to help the country recover from years of instability. As a result of this investment, Pakistan has become a leading market for online commerce, and international corporations have purchased some of its technology start-ups.

South Asia's increasing population means more energy is needed and more pollution is created. **Innovations** in technology across the region are helping countries progress. India has been developing better air and water **purifiers** to tackle its pollution problems. Scientists have also used technology to reduce the spread of disease, which is a major risk in big, developing cities.

PURIFIER: A MACHINE THAT CLEANS AIR OR WATER.

FAST FACT

IN 2017, THE MALDIVES GOVERNMENT USED TECHNOLOGY TO CREATE ADVANCED IDENTIFICATION (ID) CARDS FOR ITS CITIZENS. A SINGLE ID CARD CAN BE USED AS A PASSPORT, DRIVER'S LICENSE, AND A BANK CARD, AND THEY ARE EXPECTED TO LAST FOR MORE THAN A DECADE.

ACCESS TO CLEAN WATER IS A CONCERN IN INDIA'S COUNTRYSIDE. NEW TECHNOLOGICAL INNOVATIONS ARE CHANGING HOW WATER IS TRANSPORTED AND PURIFIED.

AWARDING SMART STUDENTS

India encourages and celebrates innovation from young people across the country. The Gandhian Young Technological Innovation Awards (GYTI) is just one example. Students are invited to submit inventions that are innovative and address an Indian issue. In 2019, award-winning GYTI entries covered many fields, including medicine, schoolwork, software, and food production.

NOTABLE SCIENTISTS AND INVENTORS

Historically, South Asia has contributed many inventions and technological breakthroughs to the world. Today, the trend continues thanks to increases in education and government funding.

Indian scientist Har Gobind Khorana won a Nobel Prize in 1968 for his DNA research. Gene therapy is based on Khorana's work. In 2016, Sri Lankan scientists Manoj Hettiarachchi and Nalin Kannangara invented a dry powder form of asthma medication. This version of the medicine is cheaper than traditional inhalers.

Many areas of South Asia suffer from uneven access to clean water. Bangladesh-born doctor Abul Hussam took on the country's water problem with his invention, the SONO filter. Easy to use and cheap to produce, the SONO filter makes groundwater safe to drink. The device helps provide clean water to millions of people living in Nepal, India, and Bangladesh.

FAST FACT

CHESS, AMONG OTHER POPULAR BOARD GAMES, WAS INVENTED IN ANCIENT INDIA. THIS COUNTRY'S GAMES HAVE SPREAD TO ENGLAND AND AROUND THE WORLD.

ABUL HUSSAM

THE DRINKING WATER IN BANGLADESH IS SOMETIMES NOT SAFE TO DRINK. THE SONO FILTER IS ALREADY BEING USED IN PARTS OF SOUTH ASIA TO SOLVE THIS PROBLEM.

LIFE-CHANGING ART

Afghanistan has millions of dangerous landmines, left behind after years of war. In 2011, Afghan inventor Massoud Hassani created a device that could detect these mines. Hassani's invention is a large wind-powered ball that moves through—and helps clear—minefields. In addition to making Afghanistan safer, Hassani's invention doubled as a work of art. The original device can now be viewed at New York City's Museum of Modern Art.

IMPACTS ON TECHNOLOGY

New inventions can make huge social and environmental impacts on the world. However, research and development must rely on governments or businesses investing money in new technology. It takes a lot of time for research to be completed, and an invention actually has to be built—and that's not free. Without funding, many world-changing inventions wouldn't see the light of day.

In South Asia, research into new technology has historically been underfunded. Even the most developed country—India—hasn't spent much in this area. However, as the region's economies grow, governments are starting to invest in technology to improve their infrastructure and education. As these support systems improve, young people will be entering the workforce with better skills and training and businesses will be able to spend more money on research and development.

FAST FACT

THE UNITED STATES SPENDS ALMOST 3 PERCENT OF ITS GDP ON TECHNOLOGY FUNDING, AND CHINA SPENDS ABOUT 2 PERCENT. BY COMPARISON, INDIA ONLY INVESTED ABOUT 0.6 PERCENT OF ITS GDP IN SIMILAR PROGRAMS.

SRI LANKA'S SPIRALATION

Sri Lanka's government understands the importance of technological innovations. Spiralation, a program funded in part by the government, is meant to help create new technology. Sri Lankan entrepreneurs can apply for Spiralation **grants** to fund their start-ups. This money can help with research and development. Spiralation also supports these businesses by connecting entrepreneurs to potential customers and investors. Interested investors can put money into research and development, making breakthroughs even more likely.

SRI LANKA'S INVESTMENT INTO START-UPS AND NEW TECHNOLOGY DEVELOPMENT IS HAVING A POSITIVE EFFECT ON ITS ECONOMY. THE COUNTRY IS BECOMING MORE MODERN EVERY YEAR.

THE FUTURE OF SOUTH ASIA

South Asia is full of potential. Economic development depends on reliable, modern infrastructure, which is being built in many of the area's countries. As each nation continues to grow, unity will help ensure the success of the entire region. Working together to build economic and political partnerships can bring stability to a region that has seen its share of trouble over the years. Providing widespread access to food and energy is also a major challenge South Asian nations must overcome. Their expanding populations demand it.

Investments in education, jobs, and technology are the region's biggest hope for the future. Local and international programs in the region are helping young people start businesses and develop new technologies. With continued hard work, South Asia's developing nations will be ready to take the world stage.

DEMOCRACY: A SYSTEM OF GOVERNMENT WHEREBY PEOPLE CHOOSE LEADERS AND PARTICIPATE IN MAKING LAWS THROUGH AN ELECTION PROCESS.

FAST FACT

INDIA IS SOUTH ASIA'S LARGEST ECONOMY. IT'S THE BIGGEST **DEMOCRACY** IN THE WORLD, AND IT'S THE WORLD'S SECOND-MOST POPULATED COUNTRY.

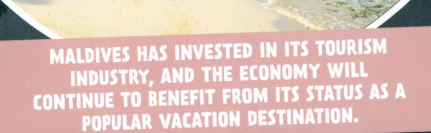

MALDIVES HAS INVESTED IN ITS TOURISM INDUSTRY, AND THE ECONOMY WILL CONTINUE TO BENEFIT FROM ITS STATUS AS A POPULAR VACATION DESTINATION.

FAST FACT

THE GLOBAL COVID-19 VIRUS PANDEMIC, OR WIDESPREAD ILLNESS, THAT BEGAN IN 2019 WILL HAVE A LASTING EFFECT ON ECONOMIES IN THIS REGION AND AROUND THE WORLD.

WATER WARS

The lack of safe drinking water in South Asia is one of the region's most challenging issues. Despite the **subcontinent** being home to nearly 20 rivers, local governments have trouble making sure citizens have clean water. Several major waterways—including the Brahmaputra River—are spread between China and India, but the countries can't agree on how they should be shared. China has kicked off projects to dam some of these rivers, which is creating political problems with India. There are no clear answers on how to solve these issues.

SUBCONTINENT: A LARGE LANDMASS THAT IS GEOGRAPHICALLY SET OFF FROM THE LARGER CONTINENT.

GLOSSARY

commerce: Large-scale trade and business.

export: To sell a product outside of its country of origin.

gross domestic product (GDP): The value of the goods produced by the people of a nation.

hydropower: The conversion of flowing water into storable, usable energy.

import: The purchase of products from other countries.

infrastructure: The equipment and structures needed for a country, state, or region to function properly.

innovation: A new or better way of doing something.

occupational: Related to jobs or the workplace.

refined: Processed from a raw material to make a usable product.

textiles: Products made of woven fabric and cloth.

tourism: The market of travel and vacationing.

BOOKS

Mondschein, Ken. *South and Central Asia.* Broomall, PA: Mason Crest, 2017.

NgCheong-Lum, Roseline, and Debbie Nevins. *Maldives.* New York, NY: Cavendish Square Publishing, 2020.

Vaughn, Jennifer. *India and Mumbai.* London, UK: Franklin Watts, 2016.

WEBSITES

Illinois Library: South Asia Countries
www.library.illinois.edu/ias/sacollection/sa_countries
This site gives readers a basic overview of each of South Asia's eight countries, with links to the CIA World Fact Book's entries on each.

National Geographic Kids: Afghanistan
kids.nationalgeographic.com/explore/countries/afghanistan
This site offers an exploration of Afghanistan's culture, government, and nature through the use of maps, pictures, and facts.

UNESCO: Sri Lanka
UNESCO's official webpage for Sri Lanka examines the country's historical and conservation sites through images and video tours.

INDEX